Candy's Pleasures

A Sweet and Sexy Guide to Enhanced Intimacy

Candy

"I can do all things through Christ who strengthens me."

-Philippians 4:13 New King James Version (NKJV)

Synopsis

Candy's Pleasures is a sexy addicting guide for the millennial woman who is a lady in the streets and a freak in the sheets! This straight talk guide will empower women to embrace sexuality and feel confident in their own skin!

In this guide, you will learn to indulge in your wildest fantasies and learn how to have explosive orgasms. You'll also learn how to have better relationships, self-love and enhanced lovemaking experiences.

Inside This Book You'll Learn:

What has prevented you from having the best sex of your life.

Tips to increase your sexual confidence and self-esteem.

Why you should never have sympathy sex & how it affects the quality of your sexual experience.

How to be more assertive in bed without fearing being judged.

About The Author

Canayec'ya J. Smith is a stylist, sexpert, author and millennial lifestyle entrepreneur. Born and raised in the heart of Louisville, KY where she currently resides. Affectionately known as "Candy," most known for her lady in the streets and a freak in the sheets persona. For several years she has been educating and empowering women to embrace sexuality and feel confident in the skin they're in.

Canayec'ya provides a straight talk, no misunderstanding approach to life, love, sex, business and entrepreneurship. She prides herself on her charismatic personality, no nonsense attitude and relentless drive. Her passion comes from helping people live their best lives and gain sexual independence and freedom.

She is a graduate from Central High School MCA, a licensed master cosmetologist and obtained her Associates degree in Small Business Management and Entrepreneurship. She is now pursuing her Bachelor's degree in Marketing.

Dedication

This book is dedicated to women who have come before me, the women who have raised me and the women that I will raise.

To My Mother, BBWB - Beyond Bitch Way Beyond:

Thank you for teaching me how to respect myself as a woman and to demand respect from others. You have always taught me to love and honor myself, to never compromise who I am, to have key values and morals about myself, and to stand firm on them. Thank you for being my first example of what hard work looks like.

Everyday, I would see you get up and go make it happen for our family. You always reminded me to apply myself and to really go after the things that I want. You nurtured my creative ways and always allowed me the freedom of trying different things I was passionate about.

I wish you were here to see how much I have grown as a woman and how each and everyday I'm growing to sound more like you. I remember all the long talks you gave about womanhood whether I wanted to hear them or not. I want you to know that your words and presence were appreciated.

To My Father

Thank you for teaching me how to hustle and survive. You taught me so much about people and to never leave the house without a set plan or mission. I also remember how you taught me to never return home until the money is made or the mission is accomplished. You taught me how to build rapport with people and the importance of doing what you say you are going to do.

I am forever grateful for you being in my life and teaching me how a man should respect and treat me. Your outlook and mindset about life is unmatched, your value for knowledge and education has taught me the importance of never being complacent. To always want to learn and desire more.

To My Sister

You are my motivation and the fuel to my fire. You keep me on my toes and always remind me to strive for the best. My constant reminder that someone is always looking up to me to teach them how to become a woman.

You will always be my first true love and my baby no matter how old you get or where you go in life. With this book, I want you to know that all things are possible when you believe and work hard. Dream big and don't ever listen to anyone say what you can't do.

To Meme

My meme was my inspiration. She was a very successful nurse practitioner and professor of nursing. She held several degrees and was affiliated with some of the most profound and elite societies. She was successful in her career, wife to her husband and amazing mother to her child and her grandkids.

I understood her impact on my life and where my drive to succeed came from. I appreciate every lesson and every piece of wisdom from her. She taught me to embrace womanhood and my role in my family.

"Be a lady!" She always said. But I never knew how hard that would actually be.

Make your own money.

Keep your hair fixed!

Dress well!

Take care of your man or someone else will!

Raise your children in the way you want them to go!

And most importantly, be a lady and keep it classy!

I say all of this to say that we as women desire to have a dream life and career, but it takes hard work and dedication to truly become the woman we want to be, and to obtain our dreams and aspirations. It truly does cost to be a boss. We sacrifice so much but we must aspire to inspire, all the while being a lady in the streets!

Daisy Judkins

My therapist. The first person who ever took the time to listen to my story and simply just be a listening ear. You never judge, but always helping me to find some sort of peace in my time of chaos. Thank you for teaching me how to love and most importantly be loved.

Karlyn LeBlanc

For teaching me the game and introducing me to your company, it was in my destiny to meet you at the Bronner Brothers hair show in Atlanta and ultimately becoming a romance consultant.

At the time, I was only twenty years old and I came to your event in Chicago and my life was completely changed. You taught me that the sex toys are only a product but you have to have skill to sell them.

You were the first person to teach me about the importance of networking, branding and marketing. Your amazing skill to motivate and empower others has pushed me to become a woman that I had known existed in me for a long time. Your guidance and mentorship has shown me what it takes to journey through womanhood while being graceful and owning who you are.

Tara Thomas

For simply being who you are, the authentic genuine soul that you are. You showed me that dreams do come true as long as you are willing to work hard for it.

The moment we met at the airport and you asked me to go to Atlanta with you changed the way I looked at business. You said, "Well you can go to work if you want, I'm going to chase this check!"

In that instant, I made the decision that I was no longer an employee but a Boss, the boss of my own life. Furthermore, if you stay ready you don't have to get ready.

Introduction

This is not just another sex book that tells you basic sex tips. This is a straight talk, no nonsense guide about how to upgrade and enhance your intimacy and lovemaking experience between you and your partner.

Furthermore, this guide will help empower you to embrace your sexuality and live your best intimate life. You will learn how to have a more positive experience with those you care about the most.

I have provided many tips, tricks, ideas and experiences that will be sure to make you wet and in addition it will equip you with the tools you need to fully embrace your inner self. I wrote this book for all of my passionate lovers out there who yearn for deeper, enhanced lovemaking and sexual satisfaction.

Everything I know about pleasure, intimacy, love and relationships will be explored in this book. I have several years of experience as a sexpert and romance consultant. Many women tend to have some of the same struggles when it comes to intimacy and self-love.

Whether we are taking care of our families or building our dream lives we can all agree that we want to own our sexuality and embrace the skin we're in. Self-love is a process, it takes time to become fully aware of who you are and what it is exactly that we want.

Relax

Relaxation plays a very important part of sex and intimacy. When you are relaxed you are more open to things you wouldn't normally be open to doing usually because you are in a calm state. When you are in the right mindset you increase your lubrication and ability to have better, more intense orgasms.

Whatever you choose to do for recreational purposes will increase your hormones as well. Alcohol, marijuana and other aphrodisiacs have been used for many years to increase stamina and libido.

The Power of Pleasure and Passion

Let's start by exploring the true meaning of pleasure and passion:

What is Pleasure?

1. The state or feeling of being pleased
2. Enjoyment or satisfaction derived from what is to one's liking; gratification; delight;
3. Sensual gratification.

What is Passion?

1. Any powerful or compelling emotion or feeling, as love or hate;

2. Strong amorous feeling or desire; love; ardor;

3. Strong sexual desire; lust.

What is Love?

Understanding is the root of love

Love;

noun

1. A profoundly tender, passionate affection for another person.

2. A feeling of warm personal attachment or deep affection, as for parent, child, or friend.

3. Sexual passion or desire.

4. A person toward whom love is felt; beloved person; sweetheart.

5. (used in direct address as a term of endearment, affection, or the like): *Would you like to see a movie, love?*

6. A love affair; an intensely amorous incident; amour.

7. Sexual intercourse; copulation.

Love can be broken down into three components:

Passion

1. Any powerful or compelling emotion or feeling, as love or hate.

2. Strong amorous feeling or desire; love; ardor.

3. Strong sexual desire; lust.

Intimacy

1. The state of being intimate.

2. A close, familiar, and usually affectionate or loving personal relationship with another person or group.

3. A close association with or detailed knowledge or deep understanding of a place, subject, period of history, etc.:

An intimacy with Japan.

One key to intimacy is vulnerability and curiosity.

Commitment

1. The act of committing.

2. The state of being committed.

3. The act of committing, pledging, or engaging oneself.

Chapter One

Effective Communication

Amazing sex begins with effective communication. I am constantly asked about how sex can be improved in many areas, and the main piece of advice I give is to talk about it. Your partner won't be able to satisfy you if he or she doesn't know what you like, what you desire and how to get it done. Each person expresses sexuality differently and how they receive pleasure should never be assumed. Start talking about your sexual desires and pleasures with your partner so that they will be better able to satisfy you.

It's necessary and an easy way to make your sex life greater because you both will have a clearer understanding of how to satisfy the other. Romantic relationships have a huge impact on your life and how you value yourself.

Relationships do require work in order for the relationship to work. Things won't always be sunshine and rainbows especially if you have been in a long-term relationship. You will fall in and out of love numerous times.

In most cases the spark does tend to go out after the honeymoon stage so you'll want to keep the relationship fun and unpredictable. Relationships of any sort take hard work and dedication. The amount of time you spend getting to know someone, talking to them, meeting the family and bonding can be a very happy time in your life. You think you finally found the one that understands you. It's like you were a match made in heaven and they are perfect for you.

Friendship should be a priority to set a solid foundation for a relationship. Sometimes people get caught up in the hook-up stage where the two are physically attracted to each other. Allow time to learn a person's character and their flaws. Even if you have been with a person for years you never truly know someone because we are constantly evolving and so are our needs and wants.

Relationships can be a very complex thing; there are many emotions involved. You laugh, you cry, sometimes you wish they would just die (LoL), but you would be the first person acting a fool at the funeral. You have to have a solid foundation on which the two of you build on. It starts with friendship, true authenticity and genuine friendship. You remember in the movies when the first grade girl would blush at the first grade boy for bringing her a dandelion? That kind of friendship.

Communication is key in any relationship. It sounds so overrated but it truly is a gem to happiness. If we don't know what we want and can't express it to our partner then how can you ever have a fulfilling relationship? This element is so important that I had to go ahead and talk about it in the first chapter. If you can't communicate with your partner about your heart's passions and desires, how can you expect them to give it to you if they don't know? This is where your self-awareness comes in at. You have to know exactly what it is that you want and how you want it. Explore yourself and all of your curves and all of your womanhood to see what excites you. What areas do you touch that make you get wetter? When you are about to cum do you like your breasts to be played with?

Chapter Two

Trust

Trust and honesty go hand and hand. If a person is honest with you generally they begin to earn your trust. Sex is something that you have to trust the person you are with to fully submit to them to experience heightened levels of intimacy and passion. Communicate with your partner beforehand preferences and ideas around sex and intimacy.

Relationships have better odds to become long term when there at least two of these components being practiced and applied at the same time. Falling in love is the easy part. Staying in love is the true test

What is a soulmate? Your spiritual soul twin. Only by letting out your heartbreak do you create the emotional force to attract your soulmate.

Compromise

A wise woman once told me to "Drink from one's cup but not from one's cup."

Vulnerability can sometimes be a tough task to complete being open and allowing someone or something the privilege (because it is a privilege). A privilege of allowing someone to enter and experience your inner most spiritual authentic self. Most people don't allow themselves the chance to experience vulnerability because of trust issues or past experiences that have caused them to kind of put a guard up around themselves for protection. Although it can be hard to let people into that space of our lives, it is something that is deemed necessary to attract and keep a happy relationship and partner. Your partner is not a mind reader and unless you are open to express your desires, they will never know how to satisfy you. If you and your partner are having a conversation and there is something you know you really have to say or something you want to do but you don't want to seem weak or selfish, you need to express yourself. Those are your true feelings and it is important for you to express them. If you don't, you will be disappointed in yourself that you didn't act upon it.

Learn how to trust your own instincts and gut feelings because you are the only one who can change.

Chapter Three

Self Love

People are so caught up in trying to have a "Relationship" that they forget the most important relationship is the one within themselves! Self-love is the best love. You don't need a man or a woman to validate you!

Being single can definitely be a blessing when you choose to spend the time focusing on you and bettering YOURSELF as a person. Women spend so much time supporting, taking care of and nurturing everyone else that we forget about the importance of SELF LOVE! You have to learn to forgive yourself for not knowing the things you didn't know. You are valuable and worth so much. Allow yourself the freedom to stay true to who you are.

Take a moment to look in the mirror and just admire yourself. Embrace all of your curves and feel the softness of your skin. You are unique no one has the essence of your unique being. Which is why it pays to be authentic.

Self care and self-love go hand in hand, furthermore you have to incorporate self-care techniques into your daily routine. No matter how big or small the act is, it counts because you are choosing to better yourself as a woman. Some of the ways that you can include self-care into your daily regime are:

1. Take a nice hot bubble bath with your favorite bottle of wine.
2. Embrace quiet time, away from the rest of the world.
3. Try a new fragrance, for yourself or for your home (candles and incense are also great!).
4. Get your hair and makeup done! It is said that when you look good you feel good.
5. Have Confidence - A woman with confidence can conquer the world!
6. Go Shopping.
7. Travel - Traveling revitalizes your spirit.
8. Enjoy girl time - Your sister circle should be filled with those who uplift you and want to see you win in life.
9. Take a walk.
10. Get rid of toxic people and negative energy.

How will you practice self-care in your daily routine and your life?

_____

_____

_____

<u>Sexual Alchemy</u>

Sexual Alchemy is the use of magic or chemistry to change sexual connections.

Clear out all of the bad experiences you have had dealing with sex and intimacy out of your life.

Be clear and set intentions for your desires and what you want.

Charge up your sexual energy and focus on using that energy in a positive way toward yourself.

Human sexuality is the quality of being sexual or the way people experience and express themselves as sexual beings.

<u>The Art of Seduction</u>

You want your lover to be obsessed with you. You want them to be so attracted to you that it is almost like they're hypnotized and you have them under your love spell.

You have to own your sexuality and your sensuality. There is nothing more sexier than a confident person, man or woman. You teach people how to treat you. Sexual encounters are all about power and energy. How often do you compliment your partner? How often do they compliment you? Sex is more than just a physical act, if the adoration is not there you should not be willing to have sex with this person because it is not sacred.

Do you really have a connection with the person you are having sex with? To embrace a deeper love we must be responsible for ourselves and our sexual experiences. Men are visual creatures and long for a physical attraction to someone, women are more emotional. Sex can be healing by getting in touch with your body, know your inner body, and own your sexual power. Positive sexual energy can change your mind, body and soul.

Teach your man to not have a dirty mind but yet a sexy imagination. There is absolutely nothing wrong with fantasizing about sexy erotic experiences.

Dating consistently helps keeps the relationship young and fresh.

Being Submissive

How do you submit to your partner?

A lot of women have trouble learning how to be submissive to their partner. Not because we don't want to, but because of how we were raised. We have been programmed to go to school, get your education, go to college, make your own money, and of course be independent. Not that there's anything wrong with being independent but a man wants to feel like he is needed

A man will treat you based on how you carry yourself. You teach people how to treat you! Be a queen.

The Power of a Woman

We have all heard the saying "Behind every great man is a great woman." Women birth this nation and continue to be the backbone in any given situation. When I was growing up my mother would call it "P" power. The essence of becoming a woman is what manages to keep the household running smoothly.

Chapter Four

Sexual Satisfaction

Great sex is a right.

Sex is more than just physical intercourse.

Were you truly satisfied? We tend to assume that our partners desire the same level of satisfaction as you do; physically, mentally and spiritual satisfaction. A lot of times we just remain content sexually, and we become happy with the same ole, same ole because you become comfortable. Find fulfillment within yourself and your partner.

Five ways to enhance intimacy

1. Cuddle
2. No Phone Zone
3. Morning Sex
4. Pre-Date Sex
5. Candles

Seven ways to enhance sexual satisfaction:

1. Role Play and Games

The goal of role playing is to experience your partner and love life in a way. You can live out different fantasies that you've always thought about or you can be kinky and bring out the handcuffs and blindfolds.

2. Be Spontaneous

Learn how to live in the moment and do something unexpected, sometimes with careers and families, and other responsibilities we can fall into scheduling sex on a certain day or it becoming a routine. Think outside of the box and just start having sex anywhere. When I say anywhere, I mean anywhere; pools, parks, schools, cars, libraries, etc. Technology has now allowed us to be in contact with someone anywhere at any time of day in an instant. Even, if you don't have a full blown out sex tape. There are still ways to be unpredictable and enjoy sex in new ways.

3. Sex Toys

Sex toys come in a wide variety of sizes shapes, colors and styles and are a perfect solution to adding satisfaction in your sex life.

Sex toys can be used as aides for foreplay, for arousal, lubrication and to build that desire of a sexual orgasm.

4. Pornography

Pornographic videos can help aid in an orgasm during masturbation. A lot of people like to live out different fantasies and begin to open up about exploring different things sexually.

5. Kegel Exercise

Kegel exercises also called pelvic floor exercises help to tighten the vagina and strengthen the pelvic floor muscles. They can also help improve orgasms.

6. Exercise

Exercise, believe it or not is a great way to get your sexual juices flowing. Increase your sexual desire, stamina and overall physical health all at the same time.

7. Masturbation

Masturbating often can help you learn and understand your erogenous zones and what ways you can learn to stimulate them. Set aside some time to have some privacy and explore your vagina.

Lubrication is just as important in this process because simply put, the wetter the better.

Get Some Standards!

What are your standards and requirements? It's always quality over quantity. You are in control of the type of people you allow into your space so you want to be mindful of the people around you. That way, you are not operating out of a place of being desperate when choosing a partner or your intimate relationships.

What is it that you are looking for out of the relationship? Are you looking for something long term or just a one-night stand? You have to set the standard on what you will and will not tolerate from the beginning. A lot of times as women we think we know what we want, but what we *want* sometimes can conflict with what we *need* in the time or season of our lives.

Why do men cheat?

Men are weak when it comes to pussy. Their anatomy has made them become somewhat dependent on it, or the need for sex.

Can a relationship survive when there's cheating?

Is cheating the end of a relationship? Some may say that their relationship became stronger after the affair or infidelity.

It may sound cliché but if you love each other you may find a way to make it work.

Many people may experience the effects of cheating in their own lives and relationships at some point in life. Keep your personal affairs private.

Getting Rid of Toxic Relationships

Break-ups are a hard thing to get over, Friendships and relationships.

Do you tell your friends everything? How much is too much?

Do you tell your friends everything that your lover does?

Never discuss how good your partner's sex is. The only thing they need to know is that you are satisfied, and they will know that by the smile on your face; the continuous praise you give for being fulfilled in your relationships.

Some people will not be okay with you being happy and maintaining a positive attitude and outlook on your lover and love life. That's why you have to have some set boundaries regarding your friendships.

Even some of your friendships will change when you get into a relationship. Some can become envious of your happiness or your perceived happiness, especially if they are not fulfilled in their own personal relationships.

People in general will change over time whether that is for the good or the bad; evolution will take place as it should. You will find ways to rediscover yourself and who you are as a woman and that may not align with what others are or whom they think you should be. It is okay to rebuild yourself and find new ways to love on you.

Chapter Five

It takes women generally fifteen to twenty minutes to get aroused or get wet and have an orgasm.

Masturbation

Having sex, or masturbating regularly can increase the quality of your life. Good sex can be overall good for your health. It increases blood flow, increases your fertility and can expand your lifespan, and we all want that right?

This question can be answered in many ways since self-pleasure is a mastery all in its own.

Have you ever made love to yourself? I know that sounds simple and very basic but many people underestimate the act of masturbation. If you don't know what you like and what you enjoy, how are you going to express what you need and desire to your partner?

Your lovemaking sessions with yourself should be intense and erotic, just as you would with your partner. Make your sex sessions with yourself special. Set the mood for yourself. Use body oils to touch, caress, and just love on yourself.

A woman's orgasm is different than men. Orgasms are produced by direct stimulation of the clitoris or the g-spot.

Your lover can either join in on the fun or watch as you please yourself; whatever suits your intimacy needs best. Recent studies have shown that women are more sexual than men. Own your sexuality.

Toys to aid in your self-pleasure session:

1. Bullet or Micro Heated Whispering Bullet

2. Cleopatra Spearmint Arousal Crème

3. G Spot Stimulator/Vibrator

4. Anal Beads

5. Oils

Tips for deeper more intense orgasms

Have a connection with who you are having sex with.

Set the intentions to have a more intense orgasm.

Breathe More.

Kissing

Kissing is a form of foreplay.

Bad Hygiene will ruin a kiss.

Closed Mouth, Open Mouth, Tongue

Body Massages

Massages are a wonderful way to get relaxed and intimate with your partner.

Ménage a Trois -Threesomes

Is three really a crowd?

Disclaimer- A threesome will not save your relationship and/or marriage.

Express your sexual desires and fantasies with your partner. There are certain rules and boundaries that must come into play when you are wanting to engage in a threesome.

The five most common types of threesomes are two girls one guy, two guys one girl, voyeur (described below), one getting pleasured and one not getting pleasured.

It is often easier to have a threesome with a male or female that is bisexual and/or bi-curious. They already express the desire to go both ways so it will be within their comfort zone sexually.

Condoms should be worn throughout intercourse and changed each time you are entering each partner. STD status should be exchanged as well and if you don't know or they don't want to share it, then you know at that point that is not someone you want to participate in any sexual activity with.

What are your ground rules for your threesome?

Is kissing in the mouth acceptable? These are the little things you want to discuss and communicate with your partner beforehand so they won't become arguments and regret later on down the road.

Voyeurism

There is something unique to say about those that admire watching others during lovemaking. It's almost like a guilty pleasure for some. You know damn well it's wrong but it feels so damn good. This is a good introductory to those who have been curious as to what it's like to have a threesome.

Chapter Six

Anal Sex

Make sure your partner is comfortable with this type of sex; Lubrication and protection are a must. Let your partner control the depth and thrust of the stroke.

If you are a beginner and have never tried anal sex I would suggest starting with a finger, a small butt plug, or anal beads. This will allow you to control the depth and speed of the motions. One of the most important things to do is to relax. Use a desensitizing lubricant to numb the anus which, which will allow for a much easier penetration.

The first stroke is usually the most uncomfortable. If it becomes too uncomfortable or unbearable please let your partner know so they can adjust their strokes accordingly. Don't force anything that you are uncomfortable with or that may be painful. Once inserted, the motions should be slow and gentle to get you used to this type of penetration. Once you become familiar with your tolerance level you can then adjust your strokes and pace as you wish.

Phone Sex

Have you ever tried phone sex with your partner? Back in the day it used to be simply masturbating, imagining, or fantasizing what your lover is doing to themselves on the other end of the landline phone. Or you could call a chat line. Nowadays with technology we have many ways to get and keep the juices flowing over the phone.

Facetime, Skype, Snapchat have now allowed lovers to take phone sex to the next level by incorporating videos and "Sex-ting Messages." I'm sure they weren't intentionally created for that purpose but we lovers have to stay creative.

Spice it up by dressing in lingerie and creating a sexy ambiance for your lover to enjoy while they are away. Light some candles, and incorporate some soft, sexy music.

Shower Sex

For great shower sex first and foremost you want to invest in a good shower head with a sprayer. You can get a nice inexpensive one at your local Wal-Mart or hardware store. The showerhead with sprayer will allow you and your lover multiple ways to get dirty and then get clean.

The power of a multi-function showerhead can change your life in more ways than you think. This one simple trick can allow you and your partner to become more intimate and experience new things in the shower. If I had to choose I would recommend getting a shower head with at least six to eight different spray settings, that way you can get more bang (literally) for your buck.

Showering with your partner allows you to be completely vulnerable because not only are you naked but also you have time to actually clear your mind. You get the opportunity to think about things you wouldn't normally be able to think about from the pressures of the outside world. Your mind is more open and you are better able to receive love and pleasure.

Take this time to embrace your partner's touch or to touch them and I mean really be in the moment. Make it intense and erotic. When you touch them start at the shoulders and just allow the softness of their skin to slide down the palms of your hands. Let your fingertips slide down their soft skin.

Bathtub Sex

Since the infamous shower rod-gate and surfboard scandal, many couples have been waiting to experience enhanced lovemaking in the bathtub. Many of us have done this way before it was cool!

Chapter Seven

Sex Toys

The top three toys for enhanced lovemaking:

1. Cock Ring
2. G-Spot Vibrator
3. Basic Bullet

Use lubrication although I know most women would say they always stay aquafina ready. Lubrication is important to use while using a condom to prevent dryness and if you go for a while you will eventually start to dry from the air. These basic sex toys have the ability to take routine to incredible. They are really small but powerful and won't intimidate your partner.

Cock Ring

Cock rings are used to stimulate the blood flow throughout the penis. When blood is flowing to the penis it makes it easier for the penis to become and stay erect. It also can aid in delaying the male orgasm and making it more intense.

Cock rings work by constricting the blood flow to the shaft of the penis. They can be used with or without a partner and they can include both a cock ring and a ring for the balls as well.

G-Spot Vibe

The G-Spot vibrator is an internal vibrator that stimulates the g-spot area in your vagina.

Basic Bullet

Bullet vibrators are a sex toy designed for women. The toy gets its name from its shape. Bullet vibrators are primarily used for G-spot stimulation. Their shape makes them easy to insert into the vagina, and their rounded tips are capable of reaching the G-spot.

The bullet can also be used as a clit stimulator, it's variety of functions and speeds make this toy a bestseller time after time.

*

Chapter Eight

"Never suck a dick you don't like."

-Nikeema Lee

With that said, you want to make the decision on whether you'd want to give your man some head. There has to be a sense of enjoyment in the dick suck. As much as men love oral sex it's up to you to enjoy it as well. Be present in the moment and look into his eyes. Have the mindset to give him great oral sex and then you will be ready to suck a dick! Relax, it's just dick. You have to have an undeniable desire to suck on the dick.

You must know what your partner likes and dislikes. Does he like a slight nibble, or for you to be a human suction cup? You must enjoy sucking the dick, and believe me they can tell if you are not into it because there won't be any passion with your motions. You could also incorporate toys. Use a bullet or other vibrating toy to enhance your fellatio experience. Toys are for men too now.

The Anatomy of a Penis

The average penis size is about five to six inches.

Testicles- a.k.a the balls are one of the most sensitive areas on a man's penis

Scrotum - The pouch of skin that contains the testicles or balls

Perineum- The area in front of the anus extending to the fourchette of the vulva in the female and to the scrotum in the male.

Glans- The "Head" of the penis

Erectile Dysfunction

Erectile Dysfunction is a problem many men face. Erectile dysfunction, or ED, is the inability to achieve or sustain an erection suitable for sexual intercourse. Causes include medications, chronic illnesses, poor blood flow to the penis, drinking too much alcohol, or being too tired.

ED can be treated but most men are too embarrassed to discuss this with their doctor. Some at-home remedies include using a penis pump, sexual enhancement drugs, cock rings, Get Hard Crème and other remedies.

Try discussing these options with your partner in a way that doesn't make them feel uncomfortable or inadequate. If these options don't work out for you I would suggest seeing a physician as a couple so there's mutual support.

Bonus Tip

How to put a condom on with your mouth

Place a condom on the top of your two thumbs and unroll the condom until you get to the ridge, then place your two thumbs towards your tongue and push the condom onto your tongue.

Once onto your tongue, you are going to close your mouth.

Put the dick in your mouth, use your teeth and lips to roll the condom down the shaft of the dick.

Once on you can then use your hands to unroll the condom the rest of the way.

__Deepthroat Techniques__

Practice makes perfect; the only way to get better at sucking dick is simple. Suck more dick! Every time you give your man head you have an opportunity to give him a mind-blowing experience. You want to be the best he's ever had. We are no longer giving mediocre head. And I say we because I have to stay up to par on my head game as well. Whenever you are sucking dick you always want to give him that extra wow factor! You want him to be amazed and beg you to suck his dick more!

1. Relax
2. Inhale/Exhale
3. Swallow

Do not attempt to deepthroat on a full stomach or after drinking. You are guaranteed to throw up and that can be a buzz killer unless you are brave enough to just suck it up and keep it moving.

You can also try to hold your breath while you are doing it.

Take your time, and enjoy the experience, and embrace the dick.

Don't think about it as much.

Allow your saliva to become your guide. Stick your tongue out to create a pathway directly to your throat. Brush your teeth and gargle with strong mouthwash. Mouthwash will help to get your mouth super wet. Use gagging as a way to create moisture also.

Educate yourself and be confident. Also, be willing to try anything; you never know what may work out. Definitely don't bite the dick, you can nibble on the head if your mate enjoys it but be gentle.

A man's penis is a muscle so it gets bored with the same motions over and over again.

Bonus Tip

Have you ever heard of grapefruiting your man? Well I myself must say it is quite interesting. Pull out your phone and Google or YouTube Auntie Angel's Grapefruit technique. This trick will have your man feeling like he is getting fucked and sucked at the same time.

Spit or Swallow

Did you know that semen has fifteen calories?

What goes in must come out, and a lot of women do not like to swallow. The number one reason is due to the taste and texture. There is nothing you can do about the texture of the semen but you can most definitely change the taste of it. Have your man eat a late night snack of pineapples or cinnamon to sweeten the taste. Semen should taste sweet.

Cunnilingus

One of my favorite parts of great sex is cunnilingus, more commonly known as getting your pussy ate. The clitoris is of course the most important part of the process. Labia majora is the larger outside part of the vulva or the outer lips. Labia minora is the inner smaller lips. Don't forget to pleasure the inner lips because they are very sensitive especially when wet. Point and flex your tongue to enhance the cunnilingus experience. Most women would love to receive great head as well, but the simplicity of eating the cat has been lost. Have your mate focus on the most sensitive areas of your vagina including your lips, the clitoris and your g-spot.

Use more of your tongue and saliva than anything else. With moisture you are able to create a gliding motion across the clitoris, which is filled with nerve endings those of which are needed to have an orgasm.

Learn your body as and explore yourself while receiving cunnilingus to find out exactly what makes you cum.

Chapter Nine

Squirting

Everyone always asks "Is it possible to squirt" and my answer every single time is yes. Squirting is simply knowing where your g-spot is located in your vagina. Once the g-spot is stimulated it creates a stream of overwhelming pleasure and clear liquid, which by the way is not urine. The fluids do come from the urethra tube which is the same place urine comes from, but it is not urine.

It is important to know that the key to successful squirting include not having sex on a full bladder and clitoral stimulation is a MUST.

Just when you think you are about to pee all over yourself that's when you will experience one of the best orgasms of your life.

Squirting is a full body orgasm that you will experience by G- spot stimulation.

Your G- spot is the spongy tissue at the top of your vaginal opening. Clitoral Stimulation is what is most important for female orgasms and the g- spot is only one to one and a half inches inside and up at the top of the vagina.

Chapter Ten

Positions
Missionary

Missionary is the most basic, most common known sex position; the traditional man on top. The position is very simple but there is so much variation that can take place with it that you may be able to teach an old dog a new trick. What I love about it is it allows the man to truly get in his element and get what I call his "stroke" right. He gets to test the motion of the ocean. He strokes and gains his momentum. While he is stroking, this is your opportunity as a woman to enjoy his girth and manhood entering you. Take this time to experience each other by keeping your eyes open while he is on top of you. This is a more intimate position because you are able to both see each other and the energy can transfer easily between the two of you.

Spice it up by laying your legs down flat for a tighter feel, cross your ankles or open wide. You can place your legs on top of his shoulders the list goes on for the missionary position.

Doggy Style

I will be the first one to say that I love getting hit from the back. It's like the cheesecake of sex to me. You know how when you finish your dinner and you know you have that dessert waiting on you? That's how getting fucked from behind feels. This position can have a woman or man in a very vulnerable state. You are (if done correctly) face down and ass up and allowing your partner to take control and handle you in a (hopefully) rough manner. While in this position play with your man's balls or use a vibrator to take care of him while he is taking care of you. This shows you are attentive to his needs and still allow him to be in control.

There are various ways you and your mate can enjoy the backshot. Add pillows or a love wedge for elevated height while you arch your back that way you are more comfortable in your posture and more steady. Use a vibrator on your clitoris for a more intense orgasm.

Ride Em Cowgirl

If you a rider and like to ride you know that just because you are on top does not mean you know how to ride. The old school woman on top is a position that is all in your hips literally.

You can practice this at home on your bed with some pillows. Climb on top of the pillows in a straddling position and just bounce up and down over top of them in a slow manner as you would when you have the dick inside of you. Begin to sway your hips from to side to side once you feel comfortable bouncing and swaying do this combination together. The two motions of bouncing and swaying will begin to make your ass have a clapping effect and I say effect for those who may not have as much junk in the trunk as others you can still give a good visual as you are pleasing your lover.

Now, once this is mastered you can add your own variations to it like rocking, spinning and sliding down on it.

Fantasies and Fetishes

Have you ever lusted for something or someone?
Sex with your boss? Sex on the roof? Sex at the park?

Fantasies are something that every individual has, about something or someone. Explore your imagination and think of things to do to spice up your sex life that you wouldn't normally do.

Roleplaying works well in fantasies because you can blame all the nasty things you do on whatever character you are playing. Fetishes are up to each individual and how far you are willing to go in your sexual experience. If you enjoy living on the wild side, express with your partner about different kinks to enjoy.

Chapter Eleven

What to have in your pleasure chest

Candy's Pleasure Tips:

Ladies, every woman must keep a sexy arsenal at all times, you never know when your bae might slide up on you! I call it the "Pleasure Chest" and here is a simple list of must-haves for your sexy night:

-Candles

-Lingerie

-Fragrance

-Ice

-Halls Cough Drops

-Chocolate Syrup

-Whipped Cream

-Bubble Bath

- Body Oils

-Strawberries

- Lace Panties and Bras (Black)

Date Night Essentials

1. Confidence
2. Sexy Lace Bra and Panties (Black)
3. Condoms
4. Black Dress
5. Sexy Heels
6. Comfortably Numb Mints
7. Fragrance
8. Lipstick (Red)
9. Lotion/Oil
10. Charger

*P. S. - Don't get caught slipping, be sure to be fully shaved and/or waxed. You never know what they will want to taste!

Playlist for enhanced lovemaking:

1. Lovers and Friends - Usher
2. Bedroom Boom - Ying Yang Twins
3. Juicy - Pretty Ricky
4. Make it Last Forever - Keith Sweat
5. You Already Know - 112
6. Ride It - Ciara
7. In Between The Sheets - Isley Brothers
8. Skin - Rihanna
9. Neighbors Know My Name - Trey Songz
10. Do What It Do - Jamie Foxx
11. Meeting in My Bedroom - Silk
12. Cake - Trey Songz
13. Kissing On My Tattoos - August Alsina
14. Bed - J. Holiday
15. Marry The Pussy - R. Kelly
16. Love Faces - Trey Songz
17. Permission - Ro James
18. Love in the Club Remix - Usher
19. Can I Take You Home - Jamie Foxx
20. 2012 - Chris Brown
21. Birthday Sex - Jeremiah
22. T-Shirt and Panties - Adina Howard
23. Please Excuse My Hands - Plies
24. Making Good Love - Avant
25. Sex Never Felt Better - TGT
26. When We Make Love - Ginuwine

27. Private Show - T.I & Chris Brown
28. All The Time - Jeremiah
29. Or Nah - Ty Dolla Sign

Conclusion

Every relationship has its ups and downs. You will fall in and out of love with the same person over and over again or maybe you won't. Sometimes you have to find yourself within that situation.

Affairs are less about sex and more of a desire for attention, love, and/or happiness. Happiness is something that we sometimes think has to come from an outside source. If we aren't happy at home or with our partners, our natural desire is to seek that void or try and fulfill that desire.

No one tells us how to express what it is that we truly want because at times we can't quite articulate what that need or desire is at that moment. We can be led into the power of temptation easily. It looks like it is good for us or we think we may want it but in reality, everything that glitters isn't gold. Betrayal comes in many forms in a relationship.

If you have ever experienced heartbreak or experienced betrayal in an intimate relationship, it is important to do things that bring back your own sense of self. Don't get wrapped up in the affair itself because at some point or another everyone in life will experience heartbreak.

You will hurt, you will cry and you will feel like you will never love again. You don't have to feel alone because everyone in life will at some point experience betrayal and heartbreak and they will grieve differently. Live through your tragedy in that moment and move forward. Your story will not look like anyone else's.